Invading God's Possible Universe

Invading God's Possible Universe

DAVID LAWRENCE

RESOURCE *Publications* • Eugene, Oregon

INVADING GOD'S POSSIBLE UNIVERSE

Resource Publications
An Imprint of Wipf and Stock Publishers
199 W. 8th Ave., Suite 3
Eugene, OR 97401

www.wipfandstock.com

PAPERBACK ISBN: 978-1-6667-0310-8
HARDCOVER ISBN: 978-1-6667-0311-5
EBOOK ISBN: 978-1-6667-0312-2

06/04/21

CONTENTS

God's Child   1

Woodchuck   3

Quite Proverbial   4

Holy Kitchen   5

Sponge Bath In Emptiness   7

Brooklyn Is A Hollow Place   8

My Prospects   10

A Bit Of The Sermon   11

Forget It   14

My Heritage   15

The Word   17

Vengeance   18

Doggy Afterlife   19

Understanding   20

Who I Am   21

I Am Not A Baby   22

Knowledge   23

Loving Your Enemies   24

Cuticles   25

Atheist   26

Stories   27

Thoughts About Wisdom   28

Holy   29

Lauren   30

Contents

God Is Not Flawless   31

God Is Impossible   32

Suffering   33

A Good Name   34

Don't Forgive Our Sins   36

Lost Son   37

Dirt Bagel   38

If I Disbelieve   39

Attached to a Dying Body   40

Heaven   41

On Vacation With My Parents   42

God Killed A Fetus   43

Susan   44

Tongue   45

Rain Seeds   46

My Life   47

Radio God   48

Arm Gone   49

In the Showroom Of Death   50

A Sneaking Suspicion   52

Inherit   53

On Losing An Ankle   54

Grandmother   55

Chatter Box   56

Love   57

Bowling God   58

If   59

Skip the Virgins   60

I Know   61

I Am God   62

Speaking to God   63

Don't Play Me   64

CONTENTS

God's Race	65
Imperishable	66
There Will Be No Comfort	67
Two Masters	68
Killers All	69
Halloween God	71
Irritant	72
Not God	73
Awful	74
Believing or Not	75
Biography	77

GOD'S CHILD

I am not writing a book because I am a book
And my book is already written.

God wrote me with his finger in ink.
If he has a finger?
I don't know where he puts his invisible glove.

I do or don't believe in God.
Something is pressing me into the margins
And making me drip back
Into the ink bottle.

What God likes about me is that I reject him.
He likes that my intelligence is stubborn
And I don't kneel down like a Chihuahua and bark.

He doesn't want to be annoyed by my selfishness
And demanding prayers.
He dislikes religion.
He settles for the spirit.

The LORD wants me to be David,
Silent,
Hands unclasped.

That's why he created me to be what he wasn't
And what he wouldn't want to be.

I go to church to recite the sacraments of self-love.
I am narcissism spun on heaven's finger.

WOODCHUCK

I believe in God's non-existence like I believe in your recalcitrant retreat from my sentimental affections.

God doesn't exist firmly like
The stiff glove with which O.J. killed
His wife.

Would God do good if he could do good like a woodchuck would chuck his teeth in the river afternoon?

Why do I argue with God's absence
Like a student telling his teacher
He was in school?

It would be so much easier to believe.
I don't.
I do.

I hope you dislike me for not believing in God and I hope you hate me for finding faith in his accidental possible merit.

Consider me Meursault in *The Stranger* hoping to be cursed at his execution.

QUITE PROVERBIAL

"Trust in the LORD with all your heart and lean not on your own understanding."

How can I trust in the escape from a doorway?
Does God exist?
Is He here?
Is He wiping his feet on earth's doormat?

I can only trust in myself because I am the LORD and I exist in my head and believe in myself with all of my heart.

You tell me not to lean on my own understanding
But all I have is the cane
Of my introspection to hold me up.
I walk three legged down the street

Wondering how radicals could blow up little girls at Ariana Grande' concert and how the LORD is so stubborn that he won't police killing or flat tire the murderous van on London Bridge.

Why does God make me juggle doubts and turn from Him like a broken ankle?
I am open to his forced opinions.
I am hurt by your insistence that I read the Bible.

HOLY KITCHEN

God shows up in my kitchen and I don't recognize him
Behind the refrigerator door.

He gives me fish and bread and I begin to get a hint
Of his power.
He has no power.
Don't ask a religious person.
He rolls with the holy rollers.
He will ascribe the might of the world to heaven.

I bought these goodies from the money I earned.
God helps those who help themselves.
So who is doing the helping?
God or me?

I don't earn a lot and I'd rather write poems than
Earn a living.

I am an atheist.
I am a priest.

Maybe I am God when he is napping?
Maybe I am a snooze?

Maybe I am not many years from not existing.
I am seventy-three.
God wants to kick the shit out of me.

Soon I will be as distant and as evaporated as God.
I lived so that I would wander with my knapsack through my wife's memory.

SPONGE BATH IN EMPTINESS

I do not fear the LORD because I would be stupid to fear my possible Savior even if He doesn't exist.
He does.
He doesn't.
I was and then I wasn't.

I respect Him.
I love Him.
He is my answer in a universe that doesn't question.

Why should I fear love when love has given me the world, a planet spinning,
A dizzying emotion, a wife?

Knowledge is my tool for escaping
From the LORD.
It is a wrench.
It is a map without a country.

I want to sponge bathe in emptiness. I want a religion without stories attached to it. I want to be the truth in a land of lies.

I don't want a narrative.
I want a poem.
I want a kiss.

I don't know what I mean but I am the definition of the wandering spirit.

BROOKLYN IS A HOLLOW PLACE

The only thing I know about religion I got from John Milton.
I had to study him in Graduate School.
Don't remember a thing.

Was it *Paradise Lost* or *Paradise Regained*?
Who gives a damn?
I am God.

I am the circle of beatification that surrounds the earth.
All you others out there don't exist.

I shake hands with my multiple personalities and am glad
To be me whoever I be.
Don't crucify me with your stupidity.
It hurts so bad.

Your shortsighted generous comments go through my palms
Like nails.
I can't walk with the rust.
I see that I am blind.

There is a borough in New York where all the people sacrifice
Their lives to regular violence.
It's a miniature version of Chicago.

Brooklyn is a hollow place where clichés of loveliness grow
Like Valentine roses.

And the slum dwellers eat each other, munching reverse bigotry.
If I were really God I would stop the violence.
I wouldn't allow what he allows when he fails to take a stance.

I don't mean to knock God over but he isn't doing his job
Stopping bullets from their attraction to shooting children.
Free will?
Give me a protective vest.
I don't want to die in a religious ambush.
I will use a Bible to stop the bullets.

MY PROSPECTS

Christ said, "Fear not, I am the first and the last, and the living one. I died, and behold I am alive forevermore, and I have the keys of Death and Hades."

Resurrection is a dream devoutly to be wished. It is Hamlet enjoying his adolescence.

Jesus Christ came back to life on the third day after his crucifixion. Did his hands still hurt? Did he still make homilies?

If Christ is the living how did he die? How is he alive forevermore?

For a modest man Christ sure bragged a lot? He did not have the humility to accept his death. He was needy of eternity even though he gave none of it to us, his children.

Christ claims he has the keys of Death and to Hades. And what will I have? A mouthful of dirt, a shovel of sadness, an end to all my miseries and joys.

God gave me a raw deal. I think he dealt me from the bottom of the deck. Heck, I will be gums from a brainless Novocain shot administered from a needle by a suicidal dentist.

A BIT OF THE SERMON

I no longer like Jesus's love of mankind.
If you turn the other cheek you let the arrow shoot
Into your neighbor's face.
Jesus wants us to not give in to temptation.
But it's only by giving in to temptation that I learned
To reject it.
I am no longer tempted because I was there,
Where I did this, done that— Dr. Dre.

Jesus says, "Take up your cross and follow me."
You got to be kidding.
Like I want to be crucified.
Jesus should be ashamed for asking me to follow
In his bloodstains.

Jesus notes, "The kingdom of heaven is at hand."
How can it be at hand when his hands
Have holes in them?
Doesn't sound like heaven to me.

Jesus shows compassion for the poor, the despised,
The outcasts.
I'm not doing that crap.
Why should I have compassion for the failed,
The guilty, the bums or the violent?
I am tired of being accosted by beggars.
I want a beautiful city.

I want the innocent to rise up in their sheets
And suffocate the failed.

Jesus says, "Be sincere, not a hypocrite."
Yet sincerity is the arrogant hypocrisy
Of failed do-gooders.
And what they do is never good.
It is a piece of good.
A failed expectation,
Exasperated hedonism.

The homeless man is at home without walls.
I was the homeless man on the poster in the MTA.
Before that I was a millionaire.
I couldn't care and I couldn't tell the difference.

Followers say "Jesus and God are one."
I say Jesus and God are none.
They are inventions.
They are the mind needing a revelation
When absence smarts the empty schoolroom.
"Don't let family get in the way of following me,"
Is misleading.
Shame on Jesus.
Family is the most important unit in the world.
Hillary is wrong when she says, "It takes a village."
Perhaps when the family is failed human beings?
Communism is always wrong.
Socialism is a mistake that gets worse.

Jesus says he "has authority over the law and tradition."
Tradition has authority over tradition
And Jesus is chaos.
Rome is dominant.

Jesus preaches, "Love your enemies; do not hate, be reconciled."
Jesus sounds like the mafia saying to keep your enemies close?
But if you kill your enemies you won't have to worry about them
And you will protect your families.
Muslims have become the Nazis again like they were in WWII.
It's time to end their time.
No more crocodile tears or the crocodiles will hide in French pocketbooks.

FORGET IT

Jesus said, "I am the resurrection and the life. Whoever believes in me, though he die, yet shall he live, and everyone who lives and believes in me shall never die. Do you believe this?"

Of course I don't believe this. I am not an idiot. You are not the resurrection. Outside your tomb the disciples were hallucinating like I did on mescaline in the 60's.

I don't believe in you. Why should I? You have been dead two thousand years and I have not had my last supper with you yet.

Whether I believe in you or not I will not live. I am dead in a while. Not far.

You mistake me for a sucker. I could almost love you if I could believe in you. But if I believed in you I would be too superstitious and too stupid to love.

What good does it do to believe in someone who walked around like God even though he was a victim of venal, stupid men?

You'd think that the Son of God could have defended himself. You would have thought that he would have let mankind suffer for the sins of mankind. Man deserved a lesson. Not Christ, O Christ, they done him wrong.

MY HERITAGE

I am a Jew. Why? Who?
I haven't been to temple since my bar mitzvah.
I am seventy now.
My religion has been underground for sixty-seven years.

I am stronger than when I was a young man.
I do fifty chin-ups and one hundred push-ups.
I concentrate one-armed curls with fifty pounds.
I am a God among men and a man
Among Gods.

I am so old.
In a few years I could be coffin-cold.

I am a super Jew.
I have a Ph.D. too.
So screw you if you criticize that I went to jail
Or went bankrupt.

I did none of that.
I don't exist.
I am the dream of a dream you never had.

I am not liberal.
I am a rough and tumble Jew.
I learned values when I was treated strictly in Federal Prison.
I like rules.

I bent to their authoritarianism.
There is no progressive ethos or strength in liberalism.
I like what I do and save the Jews who won't save themselves.

I am too intellectual for you.
I can be as gentle as the dew on borrowed sod.
You are a jump in the oven liberal Jew.
You bake yourself into your enemies' bread and wish
You were dead.
When you kiss your enemies you get sun burned lips.
If you can't hate back you become a statistical fact
Like thousands dead at Auschwitz.

THE WORD

In the beginning was the Word and the Word was with God.
The word is with me.

I am the word that proliferates as words
And flies around the cage like vowels and consonants.
I am a poem.
I am many poems.

They well up in me like swallows in a bell.
Ring, ring, ring.

I am the marriage of words and the arrangement of lines.
Read me.
Write me.

I am literature in a survival mode.
I am what will remain of our wishy-washy generation.

VENGEANCE

"Vengeance is mine; I will repay, saith the LORD."
Forget the LORD.

Vengeance is mine saith the good man
Who forecasts his enemies' future violence
And stops it where it starts.

Muslim blood every day and where are the Christians
To stop its spread and anticipate its bloodshed?

Cowardice thy name is false empathy.
Obama was the commander of retreat, leading from behind
Out of Iraq
And opening his people up to beheadings.

Obama drew a red line in Syria.
He might has well have drawn it on social relations.
He was a snob.
He was a lob in tennis when he could hit a cross court.

He lost his job but Foley was decapitated and lost his head.
Obama took no chances.
He lost his innocence and became presidential-rich.

Democrats are divots that tear up the fabric of the green.
The nineteenth hole is the radical death of civilization.

DOGGY AFTERLIFE

I am an atheist and don't believe in an afterlife.
I don't believe I should eat dog biscuits.
I bark.

I think that my consciousness will walk on heaven's
Water in pontoons.

I will be part of everything and more than nothing
In the yard of graves.

I will carry my metal leash in my jaw
And hit my ass with a newspaper when I crap on the floor.

I will be the spiritual yeast that spoons the irrelevance
Of possible consciousness as I choke in my collar.
I am a furry bastard.
I slobber in the clouds.

I put myself in a cage like a refugee.
I want to be separated from the failures of my countryman.

UNDERSTANDING

Blessed are those who find wisdom, those who gain understanding,

Finding wisdom doesn't make you blessed.
It makes you a liar.

Wisdom can't be found unless it is lost
And then it is irretrievable.

You can't gain understanding.
You have to understand to gain anything.
It is a precursor to success.

Understanding sits inside of you like a heart, lungs
A misconception.

I am blessed because I don't listen to you.
I am the autonomous truth in an abandoned garden near a rented castle.

WHO I AM

I was born an atheist.
I am sorry.

It's God's fault.
But he isn't there.
Or he is?

He is everywhere in his non-existence.
He is like a broken neuron in my brain.

I want to believe.
No, I don't.

Religion is corny like kernels on a cob.
But it's not me that I hate.

I hate other atheists.
They are not respectful.

I respect the God that isn't there
And the one that might be.

These are thorny problems when the rose has fallen.
Petals matter.

I envy the religious who pray in their churches.

I AM NOT A BABY

"Whoever listens to me will live in safety and be at ease, without fear of harm."
That's a load of crap.

God, you can do better than old wife clichés.

How many suckers were beheaded in the middle of prayer?
How many prayers distracted soldiers from raising their shields?

How can I live "without fear of harm"
When everyone on the earth dies before too long?

God, don't treat me like a baby.
Don't promise me ease when life is harmful and ends in the end.

I will miss my resentment of you when I go to the great hunting ground in the sky.
Maybe all my preconceptions will be tossed upside down?
Maybe I will become acrobatic and ride zebras?
I will say prayers in languages I don't understand.

KNOWLEDGE

I'm not scared of the LORD but I am afraid of sick human beings
following me down dark alleys with knives.

Did the LORD create Jack the Ripper?
I doubt it.
I think Jack dropped from his inattention
Like a car crash
When the driver falls asleep at the wheel.

The Bible says, "The fear of the LORD is the beginning of knowl-
edge, but fools despise wisdom and instruction."

Nonsense is the pompousness of proverbs.
Fear is allergic to knowledge.
It is a rash.
It is the acne that scabs up understanding.

I don't despise wisdom because I am the light of wisdom in a closed
museum and I admire myself like a treasure.

The light through the window falls on me.
Am I in the Metropolitan Museum of Art?
I am a Greek statue in the southern wing but I am modest,
I wear a towel.

I sell myself tickets to myself because I am the only one who wants
to see me and my exhibit.

LOVING YOUR ENEMIES

What idiot said, "But love your enemies, do good to them, and lend to them without expecting to get anything back?"

Great. Your enemies will think that weak behavior
Deserves rewards.
You will support and encourage their horrors
In the world.
What you will give you, will not get back.

And God will reward you for supporting evil.
Like God you will be kind
To the ungrateful
And wicked.

You will turn values on their head
Like letting the beauties of capitalism drift into failed communism,
Like calling rape making love.

You will be as stupid as a snowflake who encourages the evilness of the world.

I can only hope that you are punished by the hypocritical good. I hope I don't have to hear the slap of you patting yourself on your hunch back.

CUTICLES

I hang God by his toenails so that he can look up at himself.
I am a religion that dusts itself off
Like a cowboy from the bull ride,
Like love from being cheated on.
I don't know the difference between heaven and hell
Because each is a state of mind,
Not granite.
I don't pray because I don't like silent answers.
I am the hope of the future when the past spells
Its own doom.
The afterlife is a false premise after it falls onto a pile
Of dead leaves.
I am accompanied by an accordion that has forgotten how
To play.
I am the organ grinder's monkey begging for coins.

ATHEIST

How could you be sure that there is a God when you have never seen him rising from the fire in the bushes?

And then there are the atheists
Who know that God
Is an absent presence.

I was an atheist at five years old so I can't stand the Johnny-come-lately's who are just recognizing God's absence.

They boast that there is no God.
I knew that before they were born.
But now I am starting to doubt.
Maye God exists and I am just part of his imagination.

Now I am a dog sniffing
At the possibility
Of God pissing in the clouds.

The thing I hate about atheism is the modern atheists who mock their ancestors who sometimes loved God like tears on an onion.

STORIES

Do you think that I believe all those stories in the Bible?
And the big one—
Christ's life.
Garbage floats on the river and gives a bad smell to rumors.
I don't believe a word in the Old Testament,
In the New.
Who knows if there is a heaven?
I don't.
But one day I may float around in the clouds like a butterfly
And be stung by a bee.
I'm no Muslim like Muhamad Ali.
I might be preparing for my own reincarnation
Or resurrection.
I might be a continuous absence on the fringe of existence.
I might be the invisible nature of permanence.
If I am wrong then perhaps God's is speaking to me in rumors.

THOUGHTS ABOUT WISDOM

"How much better to get wisdom than gold,
To get insight rather than silver!"
That's the voice of a malcontent
Talking himself into avoidance of wealth
Because he is looking for excuses.
I have had gold.
I have had silver.
I am also wise.
I juggle these alternatives like values in the wind.
I don't need God to tell me if wisdom
Is better than gold.
I am wisdom and gold, insight and silver.
I am God.
Tell me nothing.
Admire what I am when I am not what you suspect.

HOLY

"The fear of the LORD is the beginning of wisdom: and the knowledge of the holy is understanding."

Fear has nothing to do with wisdom.
It is turning your back
On intelligence's inspiration.
I am scared to be wise.
I am dumb.

I don't believe that the knowledge of the holy is understanding because if you understood you'd know nothing was holy.

Except maybe me.
I am God's universe in the goldfish bowl of my head.
I don't know you.
I know that I am me.

Muslims want to decapitate me.
I am the only world I know.
They want to throw me
In the ocean
And to fish for their own sharks on the deck of another boat.

LAUREN

You touch me with your girlishness.
Perhaps you are a girly God.
You twirl.
You ballet.
You dance on the head of a pin
Like an angel.
If I didn't meet you in 69
I would have invented you in 70.
I am drawn to you like a cloud
In the corner of the sky.
It's not you who rained on my parade.
You were holding your umbrella over
Our heads to cover us from the storm.
You are a religion.
I study you but you will never be knowable.
You are the spiritual museum
That surrounds our painting.
You wall me in, you wall me out
And I am happy when you are about.

GOD IS NOT FLAWLESS

I don't have to look outside myself for God because he is inside of
me like Groucho Marx cracking wise jokes.
I am my own audience.
I have brothers.

God is not flawless.
How can you non-exist and be without flaws?
He is without substance.
He is all possible mistakes.

He is created out of nothing and he remains nothing
Outside of the invention of a primitive child
With a chemistry set.

The proverb says that, "He is a shield to those who take refuge in him."

Why would I take refuge in what I don't know?
I do not need a shield.
I need an escalator into the upper floors of my shopping center.
I have to find my heart among the juju fruits.

GOD IS IMPOSSIBLE

I have put a map on my forehead and planned the borders I will hop, skip and jump.

The Proverb tells me that I have planned my course
But the LORD establishes
My steps.

So I step in the bullshit of religion and the fabricated God who is ignoring his kingdom to jiggle with my course.

Do I really think there is a God?
Impossible.
Probably.
I want to respect his disappearance
And love his not being there.

Does God respect me for not believing in him and being intelligent enough to be an atheist who respects religion?

You can't have it both ways unless you find belief in unbelief and believe one or the other at the same time?

I might believe in God just in case he demands it and his punishments are omnipotent. Hell, is something to be avoided even if it is reluctant to burn.

SUFFERING

Why does God encourage such suffering in the world?
The Muslims slaughter on the regular in Allah's name.
God is not my friend.
He kills my friends.
A piece of God must be evil.
I question him because he raises the question
Of how he could allow such violence.
You say He doesn't want to interfere with His world.
I say it is the Devil's world.
Everyone He has put on earth will die
And He will not raise a Godly Michael Angelo finger
To save us.
He will fall from the Sistine Chapel's ceiling to crush us.
You say he does not save us because he gave man
Free will.
Who needs it?
I'd rather have eternal life.
You say he depopulates the world so we have room for
All the people.
He's God.
Couldn't he make us smaller or let us inhabit other planets?
Christ's homilies do not take the place of God's maelstroms.
He is a mean God.
I'm sorry.
I wish I could find the good that he buried within Himself.
I hope he doesn't resurrect his fondness for death.

A GOOD NAME

"A good name is more desirable than great riches; to be esteemed is better than silver or gold."

God has his values all screwed up.
It is a given that a good name
Is more desirable
Than great riches.

Why does He have to say the obvious.
Of course "to be esteemed is better than silver or gold."

I live to have you remember my writings.
Not you.
You are not important.

But to have the future read me and boast that I once existed.
I am not interested in silver and gold.

I want to be the great riches of my century being read and curiously fondled by future generations.

I envision a blond teenage girl who looks like my wife sitting in the back
Of her classroom, sneaking a book of my poems
Onto her lap and being amazed
That a great man like me once existed.

This is not arrogant egotism.

It is the modesty of wanting to grow into the eternal and last beyond this lifespan.

DON'T FORGIVE OUR SINS

So you think that God will forgive us for our sins. Why? They are solid like Hans Solo in a granite wall in *Star Wars.*

You say that "Death is the result of sin in the world, and without the hope of a Savior to forgive us for our sins, we are under the wrath of God."

The Savoir that saves is the Savoir that blesses the thief, the hypocrite, the murderer.

Please God, save the world from your saving. Punish us the way we deserve. Not for our opinions but for our bad deeds.

Terrorists always kill the innocent. Giving the innocent a death injection is just another minor mistake in a history of horrors. Capital punishment is generous compared to jihad. Killing the guilty is a prophylaxis for murdering the innocent.

If you stand in the rain to protest the execution of a murderer you are killing the innocent who are next on line for the murderer's knife on the A-train.

And what about Andrew Cuomo? He killed fifteen thousand people and writes a book self-praising his own leadership. Dictators have no conscience.

LOST SON

God is not the only one who lost his son. Every man who dies is a son who is lost.

The Bible says, "But thanks be to God that He sent His only Son to die for our sins and rise again to give believers eternal life in Jesus Christ."

I don't even know what sins are. So how could God die for my sins?

Put the sins on the sinning. Let me die for mine. Don't pin my tail on Christ's donkey's like a tale signifying nothing.

I do not want eternal life. I am not a believer. In Christ? I like women. Let me be in women. Maybe in Mary and I will be God, the father of Christ.

The earth has been around for millions of years and believing in Christ has never given anyone eternal life.

I reach out for Christ. He is not resurrected. To believe in him is a prejudice for things as they aren't. Faith is a stupid ideology. And yet when you are hanging from a cliff it provides a hand hold to prevent your fall. Or delay it.

DIRT BAGEL

What I don't like about Christ is all his liberal palaver.
My brain is already a dirt bagel.
I don't need to wash it in cream cheese.
I don't need his forcing his clichés up my butt.
I don't want to listen to him when my ears are turned
Inward listening to my soul.
God made me a religion reflecting upon myself.
I don't want to hear Christ's screams as he sets up
A punishment for himself.
I am the light that burns against the lantern of Christ.
I burn up the night like a billion fireflies in summer camp.
I don't need your religion.
I am the religion that you should adjudicate.

IF I DISBELIEVE

I have never believed in God and he has never believed in me.
I am chasing in the bushes,
Burning for acquaintanceship.
The apostles wrote the Bible like a novel and that was a mistake.
Fiction circumcises the joy of elevation,
Of levitation,
Of manic meditation.
I am not interested in the story of the story.
I praise the period.
I like the way things end.
If I disbelieve in God hard enough
Perhaps he will appear like a dog sled in the tundra.
I'm not looking to cop out.
I am not looking for the convenience of eternal life.
I am not looking for the eternal goo of spiritual life.
I want to die in a lonely basket of fruit at a wedding hall
After all the guests are gone.

ATTACHED TO A DYING BODY

"Be strong and of a good courage, fear not, nor be afraid of them: for the LORD thy God, he it is that doth go with thee; he will not fail thee, nor forsake thee."

How can I fear not? Fear is instinctive. It's what God gave me to protect myself. Would I insult God by giving him back his gift?

God does not go with me. He stomps on me with combat boots.

If God will not fail me nor forsake me why did he attach me to a dying body?

The joy of living melds with the sadness of death. I will be lonely when I no longer know the skew of your face.

HEAVEN

The Bible is a cheap version of *Idiot's Delight*.
Norma Shearer and Clark Cable are gone.
I am still here.
For a while.

Heaven is not a cartoon.
I am not going to romp with Adam and Eve,
The snake,
The devil,
The apple of my eye.

Will Donald Duck hit me with a bat?

There is a vast numbness.
I am going to be part of that disappearance.
I will float like a raft with a leak.
I will be God's loneliness.
His forgotten spirit.

I will last forever in the regular disappearance
Of rain.

ON VACATION WITH MY PARENTS

In Madrid at sixteen I looked out the window of the fancy hotel
And hoped to see a car run over someone
On the corner.

I thought I could will this accident into fragments.
I thought I was a chunk of God.

But the cars kept rolling on and no accidents rose from my twisted prayers
Because not to happen became what was.

This night disappointed me.
I was supposed to have powers in Spain.
I was supposed to master the religion of the corners
And break the glass in the green lights.

I learned that I was not a new religion and that no one would pray to me.
I became jealous of the Bible.

Why couldn't I invent the underlying spirit of accidental causation
And find love in arcane powers and distant angels.

GOD KILLED A FETUS

God wore sandals because he wanted to imitate Christ
And be loved by the blind men near the sea.
He went for a swim
To show mankind that it is not necessary to float
Along when you can stroke laps to victory.
He killed a fetus to show that convenience
Is more important than life.
No he didn't.
He killed the woman who committed the abortion.
And her girlfriends suddenly abandoned their cliché
Of women's rights.
And then he killed all of us every hundred or so years
Because he wanted to express the devil inside himself.

SUSAN

I tell Susan I am writing a book about God.
She is seventy possibly,
Like me.

She asks what it's about.
I tell her that it's about His absence and
Maybe his presence.

She looks at me disarmingly when I tell her
That I am the reoccurrence of God
On earth.
I am Eden.
I am the apple or the mushroom in an atomic cloud.

I am the words that God forgot to speak.
I am the poem that wrote itself on the blackboard
In wet chalk.

Susan doesn't really exist.
No one exists
Except God who is me who is the elegant impulsion
In a line of poetry.

Is language a religion or an attempt to define it?

TONGUE

I have never had one prayer answered by God.
He is bored by my repeated entreaties.

He is a question that elicits fabricated answers.
I don't know why I keep trying
To reach him.

What if he is evil and wants to cut out my tongue?
Could God be evil?
No.
But if I am tongueless I will not be able to read my poems
Out loud.

Is muteness evil?
I don't want to swallow my silence.

I will use my stumpy flesh as a baseball bat and hit
My ideas out of the park.

RAIN SEEDS

You pray to God and think that he is a sucker enough
To answer you.
I curse God and see that he likes it,
That he likes my courage,
That he respects my brazen disrespect.
So don't think you're going to heaven just because
You send your palaver up into the clouds like rain seeds.
God likes me—his bad son.
He is bored with Christ's homilies and soggy sentiments.
He doesn't understand why you respect his creation.
I wouldn't want to hang half-naked on a cross while
Women excited themselves.

MY LIFE

God died in order to bring me into life.

He was sick of being prayed to and wanted to kneel before me.

I patted his Godly locks
And prayed that his prayers worked against
My death.
And then I died.
Or would.

The day is not far ahead like a horse's nose
In a tight race.

I feel sorry that God is so inadequate.
Or maybe I am his failed progeny?

The most I can hope for is that he is a spiritual bath in heaven.
I am the sponge.
I suck life out of his disappearance.

I create a religion out of the soap suds.

RADIO GOD

So God said to me that he didn't exist.
He was lying.

Is God dishonest or just playing Parcheesi
With my mind?

I'd like him to be the dial on my radio.
I'd like to play Him the way he plays me.

If only I could believe?
If he could only believe that I deserved
To be eternal?

If only he'd stop playing that damned rap music
On his radio.

I can't find the beat.
I am the melody that drifted from the percussion.

In the studio the engineer used to punch me in and out.
I was all over the map.
I was in Somalia.

I am all about the lyrics. I hate music. I am meaning.
I am a guide to ideas.

ARM GONE

The girl who lost her arm at the Ariadne Grande concert reckons
"That the sufferings of this present time
Are not worthy to be compared with the glory which
Shall be revealed in us."

Try opening heaven's gate with a stub.
How do you compare a negative with an imagined positive?
You died too young.

You died at the hands of a bearded pervert
Who is humping your dead essence.

Did you even say goodbye to your fingers?
Did you shake your hand?
Did you fall into a puddle when your fellow Englishmen
Preferred a concept, freedom of speech, to your dancing
Alive at your school play?

Your parents are sitting in the audience with gifts.
You have been written out of the script and the glory of heaven
Has become the gory sight of you bleeding in the wings.

IN THE SHOWROOM OF DEATH

The Bible says that "even if we can't understand it Day-to-day, God's plan includes better times ahead for all of us."

Maybe there is a God?
After all the Bible has a vivid imagination.

Everyday there are worse and better times ahead. The future is a grab bag of good and bad. Nothing is definite but death.

Is that a good time?
Taxes are also definite but I didn't pay all of mine
And ended up working out in jail for two years.

I think death is undercutting from under our feet the antique carpet in the showroom we'd like to never leave.

The value of life is that it is not death. It has no resale but there is value in each thread.

My wife's friend owns a humongous rug company.
She walks on a woven pile of money,
Fortune enough to buy resurrection
If it were for sale.

When I lost my money my friends told me that I was lucky because I'd know how to earn it again.
They didn't figure that I wouldn't want to go back down into that swamp.

I was afraid of the boredom of turtles.
I didn't want to lift off the dummy shells of insurance men.
I didn't want to be snapped at by my inferiors.

A SNEAKING SUSPICION

"The LORD is my portion, saith my soul; therefore will I hope in him."
The serving spoon didn't put anything on my plate.
I don't have the LORD.
I don't have a portion.
I am Edward Munch's scream.
I have no hope in Him.
Just a sneaking suspicion that he might exist outside of my doubt
And entertain me when I die.
He will put on a show.
I will not run from the audience onto the stage and pretend
I am part of his glory.
I am not an actor.
I am the real thing or at least a chunk of it.

INHERIT

If I inherit the wind I will become the wise of heart.
But if I stop the wind I will become the oak tree.
Or perhaps a squirrel?

My roots will be wise and my leaves won't leave.
I will be permanent.
I will be the envy of death

If silence decides to make noise the sound will be me
Admiring myself in Narcissus's pond.

If I live forever then forever will die an early death.

ON LOSING AN ANKLE

You give me bad advice and tell me to fear not.
I just lost an ankle at the Boston marathon.
I fear a lot.
I rot in a Muslim religious plot near the New England ground.
Did you hear that explosive sound?
I am part of the jihadist's deleterious God theme.
You say that the LORD goes with me and
That he will not forsake me.
I hobble to his side.
I ball him out for not protecting me when he
Was supposed to limp along with me.
I don't see God missing a foot.
I would kick him in the ass for deceiving me
But I don't know how to kick a cloud.

GRANDMOTHER

When I was fifteen I prayed to God that he would save my grand-
mother. She was in her fifties and too young to die but the cancer in
her stomach was precocious.

I laughed at her funeral because
I didn't want to feel
The pain.

At seventy-four I still feel that I am the creep who dishonored her
when her hour of need was present and past.

I should have respected her death
With tears instead of stupid
Jeers.

I doubt that I will see her in heaven because I will find myself in
hell and recognize the nothingness that is the something of what
remains.

CHATTER BOX

It's not that I spoke to God but God spoke to me and
While he was speaking I forgot what he said.

I ignored him a little
Or perhaps a lot when you consider that he is God
And has giant ears.

I forgot the question I asked him
And didn't listen to his answer.

It was all an exercise in futility and what I found
I never knew and what I knew wasn't there.
Thank you God for ignoring me.

There is only so much information I can handle
And ignorance is the bliss of not being distracted

By the mundane and the interfering factual,
The gossip and the chatter in the box,
The irrelevant Word.

LOVE

I don't know what love is even though I feel it.
It has something to do with God
But that is just another Word
I do not understand.
I reach out onto the table and pick up tiles
Of meaning
That are as meaningless as the words of a mute.
I ride a donkey to heaven
To discover that there is no heaven and I am leaving
Shit in my trail.
I lift the donkey's tail.
The stink of the world makes me find time
To love my wife,
To love the disappearance of heaven.

BOWLING GOD

If God were a midget I would use him as a bowling pin
And knock him over into the alley.
But God is not knock about.
He is a wall.
He is a fence.
I use him to keep the vermin out of the high end alleys.
I want all the degenerates to score zero.
Bowling is a middle-class game.
I am too classy to believe in God.
I am the atheist who drinks beer and falls on his face,
Not even hitting a spare,
Choking on a burger.

IF

If I were God I would hate all the religions
That mankind formed around me.

I would regard Christ as arrogant and pathetic,
Jews as meek and too ready to side with their enemies,
And Muslims as a mistake,
As butchers
Who like to finger paint with the blood on their own aprons.

Couldn't the religions come up with something like nothing?
Couldn't they shape their mouths like vowels
And spit blanks?

Couldn't they stop aggrandizing me and blaming me
For all the sins of the world?

Couldn't they be me as I try to be Him and
Delude myself into holiness.

SKIP THE VIRGINS

It doesn't matter if I go to heaven because I am in heaven
On earth.
I am manic.

I rise into the trees and fall on my head.
I am an acorn being juggled by delicate fingers.

Who would want to screw seventy-two virgins?
I don't like them that tight.

I'd rather screw myself by arguing with an absent God
In a burning temple.

I am pregnant with the beauty of being me.
I should have loved the LORD but I couldn't find him
So I fell in love with a borrowed mirror.

I KNOW

I am a religion without the contextual meanings and proverbs.
I exist like a vaporous cloud.
I am God.

How do I know?
I don't.

What does it matter if I create the world *ex nihilo*
Or I am created by a fiction?

It is not that I am insane but that I am inane.
Silly to meet me and happy to be a balloon
in the Macy's Day Parade.

You will remember me by what I forget.
I am a religious construct in a yard among the girders of love.

I AM GOD

You want me to pull God from the ocean
And I put him on my plate under Tabasco and horseradish.
I eat God.

I am God even before I eat him.
I am holy, holy, holy.

The words don't mean anything anymore as I disappear
Into my stomach.

Don't pray to me.

Stick a fork into my religion and arbitrate
The grandness of flounder.

I am the water and the seaweed in a fishing net.

SPEAKING TO GOD

I spoke to God even though he wasn't there.
I created him in six days and then rested on the seventh.
I needed a companion who could protect me.
I was tired of my prayers disappearing in the air.
I was humble when I invented him.
I was the result of his power dripping into his occurrence.
It hurt when he took my rib out to create Eve.
But I needed a woman to dance with at the prom.
I wanted her to help me go formal.
I was thankful to the God that was in women and
The woman who lay down with me as if I were a God.

DON'T PLAY ME

"For God so loved the world, that he gave his only Son, that whoever believes in him should not perish but have eternal life."

Don't play me. I am seventy-three years old and don't have that much longer to go.
Eternal life is a mistaken notion about eternal death.

The nice thing about eternal death is that it is eternal. I won't have to worry about life when I am dead.

I look forward to it. Sweep me off the generous marble floor and throw me in a ditch. I once was rich.

Now I am poor. It doesn't matter when I am a snot shot from a snore. I am soar. I am between waking and sleeping. I will be a nose that forgets to breathe.

GOD'S RACE

The religion of this poem is that you can't see its spiritual text
Nor its appeal to the masses' lack of intellect.

This poem doesn't exist.
But it is becoming solid out of the air and the chaos.

It is taking form in a water bottle that I will drink
And quench my thirst for God
Who ignores me just for sport.

I ignore him back.
I am an athlete of atheism and a finish line sprinter.

I will not go gentle into that championship tape.
I will write a poem that will be read when I am dead.

IMPERISHABLE

On the day of days we will hear the trumpet and we will rise from our deaths
And be changed.

"O death, where is your victory? O death, where is your sting?"

Our "perishable body must put on the imperishable, and this mortal body
Must put on immortality."

It's one thing to wish for riches and beautiful women. It's silly to think that you will ride a red Ferrari across the yellow brick road in heaven.

Do you really think that you will drive to death happily and become immortal? Please don't play rap music in your convertible. I used to be a rapper. I hated it.

Now I hate false promises of immortality as I drive closer to the shoulder of the road. Death be not proud. Be permanent.

THERE WILL BE NO COMFORT

"Blessed are they that mourn: for they shall be comforted."

Comforted by what?
Being stuffed in a box like a shoe.
No virgins. The old lady will be there too.

Seeing your loved ones eaten by grass and bugs.
Trying to poison yourself by eating fertilizer.
A double dose of death.

There is no comfort in mourning.
Morning is the night of suffering in a confused stare
At a burning star.

Suffering is our lot, a lot
We will not be able to trot with broken legs after gunshots.

TWO MASTERS

Simplistic is simplicity itself: "No man can serve two masters: for either he will hate the one, and love the other; or else he will hold to the one, and despise the other. Ye cannot serve God and mammon."

How can we know the one from the other? I am becoming senile. Values disappear or flatten out on a plain like the disappearance of judgment.

I hate everyone and no one; everything and nothing.

If I don't serve mammon, I will not be able to serve God. I must know both sides to open the deck in the middle. Is that an ace or a joker?

I don't despise. I summarize. And read my brief history in an outline of what I did and didn't do without intention.

KILLERS ALL

People say that fanatics kill in the name of religion.

But the worst killers were atheists—
Hitler, Stalin and little Charlie Manson.
What about Andrew Cuomo in the nursing home coronavirus scandal?
He won an Emmy for that one.

I am an atheist.
Sometimes.
All the time.

But I have never killed.
I am the exception to the corpse,
The excuse for the murder.

I guess Allah doesn't exist.
The millions who kill in the name of Allah
And Mohammed
Are fools who kneel to an absent God.

They kill children, women and innocents.
They burn humans in cages.

If they killed the guilty they'd have to kill themselves
And find a way to slice off their heads before

They died and left a botched job of heads
Like coconuts
Planted in the rubble around the World Trade Towers.

HALLOWEEN GOD

I don't really believe I am like God because that would imply separation
Between him and me and I am one with God.

He is me and I am him.
This makes no sense.

I don't need cents when I am walking on the pay dirt of clouds.
Big bucks in heaven.

I ride a golden horse into bargain stores.

Or perhaps God wants to be me.

He wears my body like a Halloween outfit.
I swallow his candle and shake the fire of religion.

IRRITANT

When I die I will be a stye in the eye of heaven.
I will be an irritant.
I will be the past bundled in a swab of skin.
I will be blind.

I will be eaten by a cloud and become a piece
Of heaven.
I will bump into angels,
Not being able to see near or wide.

I will be the hole in a bagel
Waiting to fill myself up with tomorrow's crumbs.

I am the gift mankind always waited for
But couldn't find.

I am the poem that is embarrassed to be so softly sincere
But that still bangs its verbiage like drum skin.

Heaven and poetry.
God and me.
What a lovely combination like a bouquet at a wedding.

I am married to this world.
But my death is being delivered with the catering.

NOT GOD

I don't really think I'm God.
God doesn't have to think.
I am God.

Does that offend you?

It will make you feel better if you pray.
Don't pray.

I hate your whispering, begging voice.
I am what you can describe while
I trace you.

I am a pencil that sketches the earth.

I am who everyone else wants to be.

You are hanging from my ropes.
I am a helium blimp lifting workers in a parade,
Pierced by a sharp cross.

AWFUL

So you want to make me into a religion in order to have someone
To curse.

That's not very gracious of you.
That's God damned awful.

I put my finger up into the wind and I am blown down like a crucifix.
Christ has escaped.
Of course, he doesn't need to suffer for man when I am already doing it.
He is wearing PF Fliers for a fast get-away.

I eat matzah because I want to taste something awful.
The taste of you, the taste of me—somehow it's all tasty.

You eat me up like I am the body of Christ.
I am really nothing.
I don't exist.

I am invisible like God and I have no calories.

BELIEVING OR NOT

The only thing I hate more than religion is the people who practice it weaving defunct ideas.

Oh one more,
Por favor,
I hate atheists with their arrogant denials.

Does religion cross out the absence of atheists' negatives or does atheism make religion look naïve?

I am a religion to no one
And a cross
Across the street in another's lot,
A lot.

So many deaths by the religious and more by the atheists.
The Muslims are the flashiest killers of the innocent.

I don't know how to escape death when I stand on a mountain smashing tablets.

BIOGRAPHY

POETRY: Over one thousand poems in magazines: North American Review, Nimrod, Free Lunch, The Antioch Review, Slipstream, Karamu, The Connecticut Poetry Review, Pearl, Bogg, The South Carolina Review, Hayden's Ferry Review, Chiron Review, The Comstock Review, Coe Review, Cimarron Review, Poet Lore, People Magazine, Confrontation, Adirondack Review, Main Street Rag, Illuminations, ACM, Mudfish, Skidrow Penthouse, Terminus, Green Hills Literary Lantern, Writer's Journal, Asheville Poetry Review, etc.

Traditional Poetry Books: "Living on Madison Avenue" (poetry Future Cycle Press)," Lane Changes" (poetry—Four Way Books), " Dementia Pugilistica" (poetry—Mudfish, Turtle Books), "Steel Toe Boots" (poetry—Fithian Press), "Blame It On The Scientists" (poetry—Pudding House Publications). "Broken Paragraphs" (contractual in U.K.—Eyewear Publishing). Three new books of poems were published in India by Cyberwit Press—"This Book about Nothing," "I am Very David" and "Coronavirus Breaks the Back of New York." His latest book is "The Interrupted Sky" with Cyberwit Books.

Nonfiction Books: "The King of White-Collar Boxing," (Rain Mountain Press, 2012.} Optioned for a movie. And "Jail: The Essays" published by (Prison Foundation.)

Arcadia Press has published David Lawrence's novel, "In the Suburb of Possible Suicide."

He has starred in three rap albums, including "The Renegade Jew" and a movie at Sundance Film Festival—"Boxer Rebellion." There have been articles about him in most national magazines and newspapers. He was a pro boxer and started a worldwide movement in white collar boxing. He was ranked in tennis and boxing.

He has a Ph.D. and used to be the CEO of insurance agencies. His work and life have been featured in national magazines and newspapers including *People Magazine*, *New York Magazine*, *Men's Journal*, *The New York Times*, and *The Wall Street Journal*.